Wassily Kandinsky

A Study in the Rationale of His Theory Concerning the Spirituality Associated with His Art

Hae Won Shin

Buddha Rose Publications

The text for this book was originally composed as
part of the requirements for the Masters of Arts
Degree in Humanities, with an emphasis on Art
History, awarded by California State University,
Dominguez Hills.

First Edition 2007

ISBN-10: 1-877792-46-2
ISBN-13: 9781877792465

Library of Congress Control Number: 2009909634

Printed in the United States of America

10 9 8 7 6 5 4 3 2 1

Table of Contents

Abstract

Kandinsky's claim that art is a spiritual process will be the central focus of this study. This is a process which includes a deeper understanding and harmony between the artist and his environment, beyond what the artist sees with his own eyes and what he feels within himself. This study will initially view some of the historical and biographical factors which guided him to this conclusion. Then, this Thesis will view the writings of Kandinsky to determine if his statements on artistic philosophy are truly exemplified in the drawing and paintings he created. From these factors, in association with the studies on Kandinsky conducted by other art historians, this Thesis will attempt to prove Kandinsky's claim that art is, in fact, a process of spiritual interaction.

Chapter 1

Defining the Spiritual in Art

Wassily Kandinsky is understood to be one of the preeminent fathers of the modern art movement which took place during the late nineteenth and early twentieth century. His revolutionary techniques in the portrayal of art were exemplified during the period of time when he was an instructor at the German Art School, the Bauhaus.

Kandinsky became a formalized artist late in life, after spending several years as an attorney. As his own unique style of art developed and his art career flourished, he began to propose that art was more than simply painting an image upon a canvas or creating a physical object and labeling it as artistic work. He believed that art was, in fact, a movement of spiritual interaction between the creator and his creation. To understand what Kandinsky meant, one must define spiritual interaction. To form a basis for this understanding we can view a statement made by one of Japan's foremost authorities on Zen Buddhism, Daisetz T. Suzuki. He states, that when one gives up his own ignorance – his close-mindedness to what exists beyond what can be seen, then spiritual understanding is born. This is what Kandinsky did, move beyond the accepted and the known.

The spiritual interaction Kandinsky embraced is not limited to including only that which is considered religious or sacred, but also that which affects the highest or purest moral or intellectual qualities of the artist, anything of the spirit and not of matter.

Kandinsky's claim that art is a spiritual process will be the central focus of this study. This is a process which includes deeper understanding and harmony between the artist and his surrounding environment. In order to come to understand what led Wassily Kandinsky to this realization, this study will initially view some of the historical and biographical factors which guided Kandinsky to this conclusion. Once some of these elements are discussed, this Thesis will view the writings of Kandinsky to determine if his statements on artistic philosophy are truly exemplified in the drawings and paintings he created. From these factors, in association with the studies on Kandinsky conducted by other art historians, this Thesis will attempt to prove or disprove Kandinsky's claim that art is, in fact, a process of spiritual interaction.

Chapter 2

The Historical Background of Kandinsky's Art

Wassily Kandinsky was born on 4 December 1866 in Moscow, Russia. Some historians believe that his great-grandmother was a Mongolian princess. This supposed fact is said to have led the young Kandinsky to assume the attitude of an aristocrat. As this is an unsubstantiated belief, other historians believe that his attitude of superiority may have simply arose due to the fact that he was brought up in an upper class Russian family.

Kandinsky was an only child and was cherished by his parents. Kandinsky was reared in a psychologically open manner. This fact is noted in Will Grohmann's book, *Wassilv Kandinsky: Life and Work.* In it he states,

> *Kandinsky's father took the position that children had a right to their own lives, and that their relationship with their parents should be based on confidence and friendship.*

Throughout his life, Kandinsky's parents were extremely supportive of his life choices. It was this parental support given to him as a child that enabled Kandinsky to openly define his own goals for himself.

Kandinsky was intelligent and well educated; his life, filled with financial and emotional support, appeared destined for success from the beginning. His idealistic childhood came to a halt, however, when his parents divorced when he was five-years-old.

Germany. In Munich, he saw reproductions of artistic works of several of his older contemporaries who were either based in Paris, France, or their original works were difficult finding in his new geographic location. Thus, he began to make periodic trips to Paris in order to not only personally view the works but to envelope himself in the thriving Parisian art scene.

In Paris, much of the work Kandinsky was drawn to was from the cutting edge art movement known as Neo-Impressionism. Kandinsky was inspired by the works of Paul Gauguin and the Fauves, especially Matisse. Highly influenced by these artists who were pushing the boundaries of traditional art, Kandinsky would return to Germany and help to create what would later be titled Abstract Art.

Art was not the only thing on Kandinsky's mind during this period. In 1901, he met Gabriele Munter and in 1903 began taking extended journeys with her. Consequently, Kandinsky stopped living with his wife Anna in 1904 and was officially divorced in 1911. After his divorce, he lived with Gabriele Munter until their separation from each other in 1916.

As Kandinsky began to emerge as an accomplished artist in his own right at the beginning of the twentieth century, he also was seeking the love which would substantiate his emotional existence. He had grown up in a separated family and this separation, as amicable as it appears to have been, no doubt cast a shadow over the relationships of the adult Kandinsky. With the change and growth which was taking place in his external life, no doubt Kandinsky's emotions were being redefined, as well. This ongoing emotional and artistic expansion was fortified when Kandinsky's works were first formally exhibited in 1907 – he was forty-one years of age. Kandinsky's first exhibition took place with the German expressionist group known as Die Brucke. Due in no small part to the age of Kandinsky and the life experiences he had undergone, two years later, in 1909, he founded the New Association of Munich Artists. In 1911, along with August Macke, Franz Marc, and Paul Klee, Kandinsky founded *Der Blaue Reiter Group.*

The expansion of his artistic ideals was complemented by his ongoing pursuit of the perfect love. In 1917 Kandinsky again remarried, at the age of fifty-one. His new wife was Nina de Andreevskaya. She was the twenty-five-year-old daughter of a Russian general. This marriage proved to be much more substantial than the previous two as he remained married to her until his death on December 13, 1944.

Once settled into a substantial relationship, Kandinsky continued to expand upon the realms of traditional art. This took place in close association with his continued formation of numerous art associations in order that his artistic philosophy could be presented to a larger audience.

As stated previously, Kandinsky was an educated man. In addition, he was older than many of his art associates. One can speculate that due to these factors, and the air of upper class aristocratic arrogance he is known to have exhibited, he believed that he had something to teach the world about art, something which he felt he knew of and the rest of the world did not yet possess knowledge. In any case, by 1925 the foundations for him to become considered the father of abstract art had been laid. As such, he was offered the position of instructor at the now famed Bauhaus in Germany. From this position he was able to expound his beliefs that art was, in fact, a spiritual practice, and subsequently influencing students, instructors, and the art world on the whole, from this institution.

Chapter 3

Kandinsky and the Art of the Spiritual

Wassily Kandinsky's paintings, along with his theoretical writings on art, have proven to have a significant influence on the development of modern art. Due to the fact that not only was he a prolific writer on the subject of art, but his drawings and paintings were highly publicized and his method and message deeply debated upon in the annals of world artistic history. This is caused by, in no small part, the dynamic revolutionary nature of Kandinsky's art and that of his close associates. Kandinsky's art and that of several of his peers became known as, *Abstract Expressionism.*

At the point when Kandinsky left his profession as a lawyer behind, he began to focus his life on art and intermingle his understandings of what art truly signified to him. He wrote two books which were elemental to the foundation of abstract art and his belief that art was a spiritual process. These two texts are *Concerning the Spiritual in Art* (1912) and *Point and Line to Plane* (1926). In these works, Kandinsky discusses the non-representational and metaphysical aspects of art.

In his first text he states,

> *When there is a similarity of inner tendency in the whole moral and spiritual atmosphere, a similarity of ideals, at first closely pursued but later lost to sight, a similarity in the inner feeling of any one period to that of another, the logical result will be a revival of the external forms which served to express those inner feelings in an earlier age.*

In this discourse Kandinsky gives explanation to much of the art work he created during this particular period of his artistic career, approximately 1900 to 1915. Much of the art he created as an adult was based on childhood recollections and memories, such as horses and the brightly colored scenery of rural Russia, which in itself is a spiritual experience. This being such because he was understanding how what he had experienced as a child had much affected how he still saw the environment around him as an adult.

His views become more refined as the years progress in his text, *Point and Line to Plane*, he further details his premises on the spirituality of art,

> *The work of Art mirrors itself upon the surface of our consciousness. However, its image extends beyond, to vanish from the surface without a trace when the sensation has subsided. A certain transparent, but definite glass-like partition, abolishing direct contact from within, seems to exist here as well. Here, too, exists the possibility of entering art's message, to participate actively, and to experience its pulsating-life with all one's senses.*

In this passage he explains a more defined aspect of the spirituality his art contains. Thus, his art, as that of others, such as Gauguin or Matisse, is detailed to be not only a representation of what the creator tangibly sees, but also what he senses emotionally. When an artist is able to depict these feelings, then others are able to also experience somewhat similar senses and appreciate the art work from a more personal and intuitive level.

As can be understood from these initial examples, Kandinsky basically related art to spirituality.

To truly comprehend what Kandinsky was discussing in his texts, one must study not only what Kandinsky wrote but what he created in the artistic sense, as well. From the combination of critical observation of his art works, in association with his written dissertations on the philosophy of art, this Thesis will be able to more clearly conclude if what he states in his texts is truly applied to his art, thus, further reaffirming or disproving his premise that art is, in fact, a form of spirituality. To begin the study of the art work of Kandinsky we can view one of his earlier works entitled, *Der Blaue Reiter,* (The Blue Rider). This work is an oil on canvas (20 1/2 x 21 1/4 inches), 1903. In it, Kandinsky depicts a person wearing blue colored clothing, riding a white horse through the clearing of the forest. Because there are no definitive brush stroked lines, one initially observes an image lacking sharp definition. This gives the painting a dream-like presence. This is especially the case with the rider and the horse which are depicted as moving through the painting.

Hans K. Roethel in his book, *Kandinsky,* writes,

...as a manifestation of movement and as a symbol of spiritual development the knight on horseback was perhaps closer to Kandinsky's heart than any other motif, especially during his expressionistic period.

To the discerning eye, the painting is rather sanguine, reflecting, one presumes, the artist's emotions at the time and the emotion he intends to produce within the viewer. The landscape appears vast, with no one else in sight. Because it is mostly a landscape, he uses earth tones, such as soft browns and greens. He accents the painting with a deep blue behind the trees and every shadow.

Kandinsky in his book, *Concerning the Spiritual in Art*, states,

...blue is typically a heavenly color and that the ultimate feeling it creates is one of rest.

From this understanding we can conclude that he manipulated the image by accentuating the color blue. Consequently, the origin of the painting's title and history become substantially more relevant. In 1903, Kandinsky painted a picture which was listed in his manuscript catalog under the title *Der Blaue Reiter*. Professor Klaus Lankheit, an expert on this period of Kandinsky's life, discovered that the title, *Der Blaue Reiter,* had been written in ink over an earlier title that had been erased, *Der Reiter.* Thus, in 1903, Kandinsky had painted a horseman who became *'blue'* years later. One wonders whether he just changed the title or perhaps added more blue to the painting. Not only is the rider wearing blue but there are patches of blue coloring throughout the painting, as in the shadows, which could have possibly been added later, to create a mood which did not exist previously. Furthermore, Kandinsky had no intention of painting a figurative representation of a horse and rider, nor does the rider appear to be a figure from a fairy tale. Therefore, it can be concluded that Kandinsky chose this method of painting as a means to depict his budding belief that spirituality is present in art. He did this by altering correct time placement, meaning one can only guess to as what year or century he is depicting in this painting, and leaving the central figures of the painting, the horse and rider, relatively abstract and not idealized in any way, thus, giving way to a more subtle image where in the mind of the viewer could be drawn reflecting the work as opposed to simply detailing an image that the viewer would not need to ponder. The horse and rider are acting as Kandinsky's messengers of spirituality. Thus, this adds preliminary illustrative substance to his claim that art is rooted in spirituality.

In 1910, seven years after Kandinsky created, *Der Blaue Reiter*, he began writing the book, *Concerning the Spiritual in Art.* It is from this book that the world was first exposed to Kandinsky's theory that spirituality is directly associated and interlinked with art. He formulates general rules of subjective feeling which he has derived from self-observation. This book is an attempt to formulate the metaphysics of the inner feelings.

In the text he stresses that spiritual happiness is more important than material happiness. Such a statement is of course easier for one to verbalize when one, such as Kandinsky, is familiar with material happiness. It would be much more difficult for an individual who has never known material happiness to make such a statement. Nevertheless, it can be surmised that he made this statement due to the fact that prior to his submerging himself in the art world, he was not only a lawyer but an economist as well. Having experienced the material wealth of his childhood, which then led him into a prominent university, where he had the opportunity to study peasant law, he was able to witness their lives, lives which were outwardly simplistic, compared to the modernized environment Kandinsky lived in, yet internally as abstract as any modern society. This same idea is what he wanted to reveal in his art work.

Kandinsky, in his book, *Concerning the Spiritual in Art*, opposes the idea of art for art's sake, denouncing the forms of creativity that are concerned with means alone. Kandinsky believed that art should be more than a superficial representation of man and nature. He believed it is important to not only capture the superficial appearance of the object, but also its inner essence or soul, which the artist recognizes when he takes the time to listen to the laws of harmony which he carries within himself.

This understanding is what Kandinsky accomplished in *Der Blaue Reiter* and what he continued to accomplish in his later art works. This same ideal is what is predominant within the art community at present, with the content of an art work superseding the subject matter, as can be seen in *Neo-Expressionism* or *Performance Art.*

Kandinsky believed that art acts as the tool by which the individual is able to express his deepest spiritual emotions. It can be inferred that Kandinsky believed that though nature possesses all the majestic beauty of God, and as an individual's emotions can be guided by one's interaction with nature, this interaction is a basis for spirituality, but it is not a method for one to truly express what is hidden within. However, when nature is depicted on a canvas by the artist, it should become the same as a form of meditation, freeing the individual and allowing the individual's emotions to flow out as the images are depicted. The objective is to not copy what the eye see, but what the soul envisions.

Kandinsky believed the spirit can be strengthened and developed by frequent exercise. This theory of Kandinsky's was similar to one exercising the physical body. He believed that the practice itself becomes a spiritual experience. *'The spirit'* or *'Geist,'* in German, can be translated not only as spirit or soul, but also as mind, intellect, imagination, morale or essence. Kandinsky's use of the word includes all these meanings.

Kandinsky as a dualist, recognizing a polarity between matter and spirit, does not think of them as aspects of the same whole. However, he transcends this polarity between spirit and non-spirit by shifting the center of gravity from familiar objects for simple shapes or forms, which is used in his analyses.

Kandinsky's concept that objects contain meaning and are more significant than an empty void is based on his Western approach to spirituality. For if we compare this theory to that of the Asian concept of metaphysical understanding, we see that the Asian philosophic mind views space that is empty as the true realm where spirituality exists. The place that is created by man is more of a substance in which to ground mystical existence than a representation of it. This fact can be seen in a passage taken from the ancient Chinese text, *Tao Te Ching*. In it, the translator, Gia-Fu Feng states,

> *Thirty spokes share the wheels hub. It is the center hole which makes it useful. Shape clay into a vessel; it is the space within which makes it useful. Cut doors and windows for a room; it is the holes which make it useful. Therefore profit comes from what there is; usefulness from what is not there.*

With his approach to Western mysticism at its heart, Kandinsky continued on his path to indoctrinate the art world with his beliefs. In 1910, the same year he began writing *Concerning the Spiritual in Art,* Kandinsky was not only writing his doctrine on art, but was a key player in the movement which moved modern art forward another step towards embracing free expression as opposed to being dominated by traditional trends. Of all the forms of abstract painting there is scarcely one that he himself did not initiate.

These factors were, of course, driven in no small part by his personality, his advanced age, compared to those he associated with, and, mostly, by his previously gained abilities and experience as a lawyer, a profession in which he learned to sway the attitudes and beliefs of others. At this point in his life he embraced art instead of the law. Thus, he developed his belief that art was enhanced by the introduction of spirituality into its methods and used his powers of persuasion to relay this thought to the minds of others.

This period of Kandinsky's life has become delineated as the Munich Period. It lasted from 1908 to 1914. During this time he also believed in the doctrines of *Theosophy* and was greatly influenced by the spiritualism of Madame Blavatsky. Concerning *Theosophy,* Pupul Jayakar in his book, *Krishnamurti,* states,

> *The Theosophical Society was based on the tenets of a Universal Brotherhood of humanity, which sought to study ancient wisdom and to explore the hidden mysteries of nature and the latent powers of man. It*

established an occult hierarchy drawing from the Hindu and Buddhist traditions, in particular the Tibetan tantric texts and teachings.

This time in his life played a crucial part in the advancement of his art work. Just before this time period, from 1897 to 1898, he also studied at Anton Azbe's private academy. Azbe's teachings stressed the use of pure color, as well as the development of individual talent, so that Kandinsky was able to follow his personal preoccupations at that time – the translation, through his own work, of the memories and obsessions of his early life in Russia.

Scientific discoveries during this period also confirmed Kandinsky's questioning of the nature of the reality depicted by painting. They revealed that nature transcends beyond what one sees with one's physical eyes. It proved that life is much more intricate and complex than the average person can conceive, just as Kandinsky had wanted others to understand. This knowledge, along with his use of vibrant colors and the creation of a personal esthetic, is what makes this period of his art work differ from that of his previous style. Munich is where Kandinsky forged his esthetic and philosophical concepts. It is also where he experimented with *Neo-Impressionism* and *Fauvism,* which would lead him into progressive exaggeration of the features of the landscape, to the final breakthrough to abstract art. Abstraction also acted as a new way in which to express spirituality through his art.

This change was the result of the years of continually creating and experimenting along with the artistic atmosphere which surrounded him. Therefore, there is continual progression during this period. It was at the end of the Munich period, 1914, in which his aim was to deal with a problem which vitally concerned the man and the artist, the source and progress of his existence, the new assessment of time and space.

With all these ideas in mind, Kandinsky painted *Lyrically,* (oil on canvas, 37 x 51 1/4 in.), 1911. Just as in *Der Blaue Reiter,* one witnesses the same subject matter which is that of the horse and rider. This painting is, however, more expressionistic in style than *Der Blaue Reiter,* and his style of painting has changed significantly. Here, the subject matter is painted large and in the center of the frame. It looks much more like a sketch than a complete drawing; Kandinsky has used the fewest lines possible in depicting both the horse and its rider. The colors he chooses to use is also more expressionistic, rather than descriptive. He has pushed the boundaries of art yet further to express his emotions. Here, Kandinsky emphasizes that line, rather than color, reveals the under-lying abstract structure of the object. For centuries art theorists have held that line embodies structure, whereas color embodies feeling.

This fact had much to do with his early recollections of vibrant color and what he was taught at *Anton Azbe's Art School*. With this particular usage of line and color in *Lyrically*, the subject matter is not sedentary within the frame, but rather, the viewer witnesses the motion of the man riding the horse, as there is movement within the lines themselves. It is not a nervous movement as can be found in a Vincent Van Gogh, but rather, a smooth shift of the subject matter to a slant which infers movement. The characterization of the horse is reduced to a few lines which, by the way they are drawn, create the impression of swiftness and momentum. And the process of painting the picture would seem to have been as rapid and as tense as the artist's highly strung emotions, communicated spontaneously on his canvas. This is the essence in which Kandinsky wanted to reveal in this painting.

Kandinsky produced a second, *Lyrically,* in a color woodcut, (5 3/4 x 8 I/2 in.), within the same year as the original. It is the same image produced in a different medium. They appear to be exactly the same, but after close examination, the two works are entirely different. Here, he is not only able to manipulate line and color, but he is also able to manipulate further the medium, the wood block. There is more detail in the lines; all the lines in the woodcut have more character, variety, and the mane and the mouth of the horse, as well as the back of the rider are more expressive. Part of the change is due to the fact that Kandinsky could express his emotions by manipulating the width and depth of each cut, rather than just using the brush on a two-dimensional surface. This in turn enables him to describe his spiritual and emotional state physically through the way in which he carved the wood.

Within the same year, 1911, Kandinsky also painted, *All Saints I,* (13 5/8 x 16 in.), which is oil on glass. He employed the traditional technique of painting on glass which was still being done by farming families in Murnau. They were used as Catholic votive offerings, most often representing Christian saints.

Because of the traditional use of the glass, this religious idea of a Catholic offering would have been emphasized in any painting Kandinsky chose to paint upon the glass, whether it was religious or not. However, because most of his paintings were either religious or spiritual in nature, the glass medium was clearly a perfect choice for the artist, and which he chose on numerous occasions during this period.

This painting is a mosaic of color. The colors Kandinsky chose to use are in sharp contrast to the subject matter of the painting, a funeral. The scene is filled with various figures; there is a large head blowing a trumpet in the upper left hand corner, in front of a castle, and there is also a small crucifixion in the background, on top of a hill. Again, the scene includes a rider on a white horse, as well as a king, and others with halos above their heads. There is one figure, closest to and similar to the deceased, who does not have a halo above her head. Art historians, such as Hans K. Roethel, believe the painting depicts a gathering of Russian saints. The knight on horseback is Saint George; behind him, in profile, is Saint Vladimir. The two saints embracing, represent the princely martyrs Boris and Gleb. Due to the fact that Wassily Kandinsky was of Russian heritage, it is most likely that this painting on glass is such a depiction.

There is also no perspective within this painting to indicate space; it is a timeless gathering of human figures who are not shown in proportion to one another. Yet the painting, with all its disregard of time, space, and action, is more than a quiet grouping of male and female saints. Inspired by *the Revelation of St. John* which, according to liturgy, had to be read during the *All Saints' Day Mass,* Kandinsky combined here the representation of saints and martyrs with the idea of salvation.

It is not necessary for the painting to have been painted in perspective because there is already a wealth of information within the scene for the viewer to absorb, and the main objective for Kandinsky was to convey the idea of Salvation. The lack of perspective allows Kandinsky to divide the painting in half. Within the left hand section of the painting, he paints the sun; underneath it he paints the white dove. Within the right hand section of the painting, he paints the moon; underneath it he paints a peacock and butterfly, which hover over the deceased body. Thus, the left hand side is bright and cheerful, whereas the right hand side is dark and somber. It is similar to the way a child depicts a scene, with the colors corresponding to the emotion: black for sadness and white for happiness.

Also, in paintings on glass in general, the subject seems to dissolve into the background, and the superimposed forms enable the picture to be perceived in different ways. This provides the viewer with viewing the piece, such as lighting. A dark background will have a different effect than a light background, just as a strong light will have a different effect than a weak upon the piece. The various possibilities will change the viewer's perception.

The frame, in this case, is significant because Kandinsky painted the frame to match the painting. The frame becomes an integral part of the work of art; it is an extension of the painting, rather than just a framing device. Because the frame extends beyond the painting and into the tangible realm of the viewer, it has engaged the viewer into being an active participant of not only the scene, but of salvation.

Kandinsky was not creating art to receive societal approval. He was attempting to show people the need for spirituality in order to better their lives and he did so with his own personal methods. This had much to do with the way in which he visualized his paintings before he painted them.

During his time at the Bauhaus, from 1922-1933, Kandinsky was able to use this talent of visualization and further experimented in making visual the spirituality found within art and teaching his students to do the same. He worked out a precise idiom of his own, a formulation of points and lines, which in turn created curves, circles and geometric shapes. These elements are at the same time an instrument of research and a means of expression. This period was a time of tremendous self analysis for Kandinsky. Throughout it, he was experimenting and refining his own understanding of his art.

At the Bauhaus, within its creative surroundings, he was able to experiment without defined boundaries and then expound his newly developed understanding to his students. Thus, they could be led down a path of artistic idealism founded by Kandinsky.

Concerning his teachings at the Bauhaus, Kandinisky wanted to teach the students to experience objects as living entities, to observe the forces and tensions between objects. To him each figure consisted of a system of forces, attracting, repelling, moving in various directions or remaining immobile, a system which had to be in equilibrium. In this sense, the elements constituting such a complex are alive because the power to exert and resist force are attributes of living things.

This ideal of equilibrium was not a new one to him, as can be seen in his earlier work,

Lyrically. In general, this is the natural way in which one views a work of art; the viewer senses when a work is in equilibrium or not, comparing it with nature. One does not necessarily need to be an art critic to sense imbalance within a work of art.

Overall, Kandinsky was a different type of teacher and many of his views differed from his colleagues at the Bauhaus. His views differed immensely even with that of his closest friend, Paul Klee, whom many art historians do not fail to mention when speaking of Kandinsky. While Klee formulated his trains of thought with caution, continually pointing out that whatever was right for him was not necessarily true for others, Kandinsky presented the end results of his deliberations, precluding the possibility of other standpoints. Therefore, while Klee pursued the truth through all possible forms of the appearance of things, Kandinsky dictated laws, with the same conviction as a lawyer does.

With this in mind, when one views, *Composition VIII,* (oil on canvas, 55 1/8 x 78 3/4 in.), 1923, during his early years at the Bauhaus, one sees an extreme transformation from such earlier works as *Der Blaue Reiter* and *Lyrically*. This is a work of complete abstraction; the viewer is left with only lines, curves, and geometric forms and an array of color. Some of the floating forms look like stained glass pieces which have shattered off a church and are now not merely floating or lying flat upon the canvas, but are attracting and repelling one another in the air. There is a tension within the objects themselves.

Just as Kandinsky intended to show the forces among objects, the shapes appear to have been pulled and stretched. A 19th Century English scientist, Sir Francis Galton, writes about individuals who control their mental images and are able to construct elaborate geometric structures piece by piece within their mind. This describes the kind of mental process that enabled Kandinsky to produce this work because it may not seem like it at first glance, but the placing of each form is organized in such a way that there is an equilibrium within the painting.

It is difficult for the viewer to describe what one is viewing because it is created from Kandinsky's inner-self. In fact, Kandinsky attempts to guide the viewer to this point. This can be found stated in Kenneth C. Lindsay's book, *Kandinsky: Complete Writings on Art*, where Kandinsky is purported to have stated,

> *The observer must learn to look at the picture as a graphic representation of a mood and not as a representation of objects.*

It is difficult to observe in this particular painting that he believed that realistic and abstract art are equal in quality. Most importantly, he believed the artist should decide what was *'internally necessary'* for him and then choose from the different abstract shapes, lines and colors.

It may not appear as such, but his feelings at the time he created this work are what he has *'outlined with a penci'* upon the canvas. One is experiencing another universe, a universe which existed within Kandinsky's own mind. And because Kandinsky believed art was equally as important as nature, this means that his art work, such as, *Composition VIII,* has as much significance as any object found in nature.

As one continues to view *Composition VIII,* one notices the large circle radiating in the upper left-hand corner is the most powerful because of the size and color. It is important to realize that the circle was of great importance to Kandinsky. The circle represents somewhat of a contradiction. Kandinsky states, *"The circle represents the cosmos, but is at the same time the most modest of forms; it is precise but variable; stable and unstable."* He believed the circle was the closest of the three primary forms to the fourth dimension. He may have had this belief because when one views a circle Kandinsky has painted, for an extended amount of time, it no longer remains a two-dimensional shape depicted upon a canvas, but rather what the viewer chooses to make of it.

Though Kandinsky did not want viewers to focus on the use of shape, such as the circle, it is difficult not to. Also, the circle in the form of a wedding ring represents infinity because there is no beginning and there is no end. This, Kandinsky must have thought of as well, and therefore, had further attachment to this form, aside from the fact that he was married twice. To many, the circle represents similar meaning to that of Kandinsky. Thus, the circle in his art work may be perceived in the same way in which Kandinsky intended it to be appreciated. This is what he was seeking, a spiritual experience by the viewer.

Changing from the horse to the circle was a natural transition for Kandinsky. Both are found in nature, but whereas the horse represents limited ideas, a circle has limitless possibilities and conjures up countless ideas within the viewer. The circle also represents a transition spiritually, in that the horse stemmed from his childhood, acting as an abstract idea, whereas the circle and its importance submerged as an integral part of his art when he had further experimented and was analyzing and deconstructing every part of a picture. The circle may be a representation of the horse and rider as a whole, as an abstract shape.

This painting is also a perfect illustration of one of Kandinsky's most controversial sayings, as it is found in Michel Conil Lacoste's book entitled, *Kandinsky*:

> *'The contact of the acute angle of a triangle with a circle is no less powerful in its effect than that of the finger of God with the finger of Adam in Michelangelo's painting.'*

To this end it can be understood that for Kandinsky geometric forms replace natural forms: God is represented as a triangle and Adam is represented as a circle. Kandinsky does this because natural forms obstruct the viewer from seeing the spiritual aspect of the painting. With geometric forms, it is difficult to identify the forms with predetermined ideas and memories, thus one is left only with the inner, spiritual quality, which this work contains. Of course, the viewer also has a particular feeling when one envisions the sharp corner of a triangle piercing a circle. Again, the shapes Kandinsky creates become abstract representations of what the viewer allows it to be.

Kandinsky believed artists are messengers from God. He believed that the gift an artist possesses is extremely powerful. Possibly, he believed that nature is equal to art because just as God created nature, artists create art. This statement may seem blasphemous, but Kandinsky never abandoned the Russian Orthodox faith of his youth. It left a lasting impression upon his entire artistic career, which was a quest of the spiritual, of the inner truth behind external appearances. To him the aims of religion were the same as the aims of art. They were, as he said, *"Both parts of the same great tree."*

Composition VIII is an example of a *'Composition,'* a label which serves to indicate the degree of spontaneity of its conception, as well as its origin. *'Compositions'* are the results of a series of studies and sketches to the final polished work. This is in comparison to *'Impressions,'* which give a new interpretation to the outside world, in which one can still recognize the original landscape. Therefore, similar to works done by

Pablo Picasso, whom Kandinsky admired, this work may have started originally with natural forms and later reworked and transformed by Kandinsky to the present piece.

Composition IX, (oil on canvas, 44 7/8 x 76 3/4 in.), painted in 1936, is another highly abstract painting. This time there are not as many geometric shapes filling one space. Kandinsky has also added some geomorphic shapes. He has painted five diagonal lines in the background, each separated by a different color, the placement of which contains much significance. Kandinsky believed horizontal lines represent a cool tranquility whereas vertical lines characterize a warm tranquility. Kandinsky also believed that when forms move upwards on a cool basic plane, as can be witnessed in, *Composition IX,* it will have a dramatic effect.

This is because the black border acts as an outline, emphasizing the direction of the stripes. Beyond, line and color, he also analyzed placement of objects, in order to express himself. Every detail of this painting and his other paintings has been extremely calculated with his given rules. There is a reason for every line's placement, since each placement has a particular effect upon the viewer. Kandinsky believed that just as every living being has a natural sense of 'up and down,' the basic plane – as an organic being also has a definite relationship toward the direction, up and down. Also, as Hans K. Roethel writes in his book, *Kandinsky,*

The left side of the basic plane causes weaker, yet similar sensations as does the movement toward the upper line; it also evokes lightness, looseness, and the feeling of liberation. The colors and the tonality of Composition IX are convincing illustrations of Kandinsky's theories: it is typical of the artist's intricate manner of composing a work that the configurations on the yellow triangle at the left seem to represent a counterweight to its 'natural' lightness.

Furthermore, because of the diagonal lines, the other forms appear to both float and rest upon the canvas. Here, unlike, *Composition VIII*, where most of the colors fade off into a different color, having an air-brushed effect, he has used more saturated colors, which provide the painting with a higher intensity. It demands more emotion from the viewer.

Similar to the large dark form which dominates the viewer's attention in *Composition VIII*, the large geomorphic black form in the center of, *Composition IX,* is emphatic. The black form here looks like a tunnel or transport through which the other smaller forms may pass. It is not as perfect and symmetrical as the circle in, *Composition VIII*. This shape has movement, rather than being static.

When one views this particular work of art, one is reminded that Kandinsky was also a musician. He began taking piano and cello lessons in 1876, at the age of ten, and later as an adult formed a long-lasting friendship with

Arnold Schonberg. With this in mind, one witnesses Kandinsky's comparison of, *Composition VIII*, with a piece of music in Gillian Naylor's book entitled, *The Bauhaus*.

> *Music, he writes, is the art which 'is completely emancipated from nature, [and] does not need to borrow external forms from anywhere in order to create its language.' 'Hence the current search for rhythm in painting, for mathematical, abstract construction, the value placed today upon the repetition of color tones, the way colours are set in motion, etc.' These experiments are only viable, however, in so far as they respond to the laws of 'inner need' and to 'inner nature', expressed through form and color which are subject to their own laws. Music, like art, has its own evolving laws and grammar, and even Schonberg whose 'music leads us into a new realm, where musical experiences are no longer acoustic, but purely spiritual' recognized that there was no such thing as absolute freedom.*

In this statement, Kandinsky is saying that without the spiritual quality and intent of the artist, an art work would miss the added dimension and appear merely decorative, which is what Kandinsky abhorred and did not intend to create when he painted. Kandinsky had realized his own laws and rules in art, which worked for him and was able to spread spiritual ideas to others. This painting most closely represents, visually, what one would feel emotionally when listening to a piece of classical music; colorful, free-floating, non-describable forms. Sometimes it is difficult to explain what one feels within oneself, but these forms seem to express those feelings, and he chose to use symbols largely divorced of representative significance, as in a musical composition. He knew that no line or form could be drawn which did not carry some meaning and that every color had its psychological effect. He proceeded to compose with these *'abstract'* forms and colors, by manipulating their psychological effects, to reproduce his past personal experiences.

His hope was that others would appreciate his work and what he was attempting to convey, for it is rare that an artist creates only for his own viewing, especially with all the analysis involved in Kandinsky's art work. Yet, he wanted those who viewed his work to do more than to just look at the work; he wanted the viewer to see beyond the physical quality of the art work and to allow the feeling he had put into the work to effect the viewer. This he knew was a difficult task because he believed that often times the spirit is concealed within matter to such an extent that it is difficult for most individuals to perceive. For him it was easier because he had exercised his gift. Kandinsky possessed the power of complete visual recall; sometimes, particular external impressions could trigger off the reproduction of a past experience in all its original intensity. Likewise, under the influence of certain stimulus, his imagination could produce subjective impressions of a visionary kind – spontaneous experiences which had the same intensity as the experience of external reality. From this, Kandinsky realized that, although there is a distinction between them, the inward reality of the mind can be experienced as concretely as objects of the outer reality. This realization had a significant influence on the progressive development of his art work. This provided the artist with a clearer understanding of his talent and subsequently, he was able to use it to its fullest extent.

This understanding is what one witnesses when viewing one of Kandinsky's later works, *Sky Blue,* (oil on canvas, 39 3/8 x 28 3/4 in.), painted in 1940. When one first views this painting, one understands the Kandinsky quote which was revealed in Kenneth C. Lindsay's book, *Kandinsky: Complete Writings on Art.* He stated,

> *The inclination of blue toward depth is so great that it becomes more intense the darker the tone, and has a more characteristic inner effect. The deeper the blue becomes, the more strongly it calls man toward the infinite, awakening in him a desire for the pure and, finally, for the supernatural.*

Kandinsky envisioned the color blue as a spiritual color. Along with the use of the color blue, just as in many of Kandinsky's other paintings during this time period in his life, one witnesses more of the geomorphic forms which have now become highly intricate in themselves. They have more dimension and appear to take on a life of their own, coinciding with Kandinsky's own spiritual development. In Paul Overy's book, *Kandinsky: The Language of the Eye*, Kandinsky states,

> *All the forms which I ever used came 'from themselves`, they presented themselves complete before my eyes, and it only remained to me to copy them, or they created themselves while I was working, often surprising me. with the years, I have now learned somewhat to control this creative power. I have trained myself not simply to let myself go, but to bridle the power working within me, to guide it.*

To Kandinsky, his creative power taking control must have been similar to doodling, where the hand creates as rapidly as the mind thinks. In this particular piece, the forms begin to almost take on forms which can be found in nature. One looks like an octopus, another like a snake, and yet another like a chicken. Although, Kandinsky discouraged viewers from seeing suggestions of objects and figures in his work because he was afraid people would confuse them as descriptive. Yet many of the forms in his last works contain dream-like suggestive connotations.

It is inescapable for an artist, especially for an artist such as Kandinsky who had painted for decades, to be able to hide suggestive connotations any longer, subconsciously, even with his over-analysis of a work of art. In actuality, this is what has almost disappeared in his later works or this time period is the over analysis and one senses more of a freedom. *Sky Blue* is a whimsical piece, with each brightly colored and designed form happily floating in a blue monochromatic background. Now, space is of great significance, and one senses a certain surrealistic quality because of the use of space, but, even though Kandinsky used abstract expressive means that were subtly surrealist, these means show a different inner dimension compared with the intentions and dreamlike methods of Surrealism. This is because surrealism contains a continuous thread of alarms from the representation of nudity, which is dreamlike and unhealthy in Delvaux's paradox to the de-mystifying possibilities of the world of Dali.

On the contrary, Kandinsky's forms are not alarming at all. They look like the images witnessed when one closes ones eyes and sees the blood cells moving underneath the eyelids. His work contains a spirituality which the art work of many of the surrealists did not contain. Many surrealistic works of art are contradictions of spirituality because they are depictions of amorality or contain a dark side to them, as in the works of Salvador Dali. Dali's famous oil and collage (1929), entitled, *Lugubrious Game*, in particular, with his use of vibrant colors and a beautifully blue colored sky can not cover up the fact that it is a dark piece. This is considered to be a dark piece, not by the usage of color, but rather, by content. There is nothing spiritual in the explicit imagery of masturbation and excrement, which is the main focus and content of this work. In comparison, none of Kandinsky's paintings can be considered dark, even with his particular usage of black in some of his other paintings and how the color black had negative mental associations for him, stemming back from his childhood. That was not what he was attempting to convey. There is a lightness to his work: this is the spiritual essence one senses is emanating from his work, which can not be found in Dali's paintings, as esthetically beautiful as they may be visually.

Jelena Hahl-Koch explains how the last, Paris canvases, such as, *Sky Blue*, reveal the true essence of all painting and all art. They accomplish this by disclosing its true theme, which is the mystery of life. Through these colors and forms, they define the means of achieving that revelation, because when the reality of their pure subjectivity is lived and experienced, they are themselves a part of life. This is a simple, yet eye-opening explanation which serves to explain the reasoning behind Kandinsky's later art, and how the experiencing of the art work created during this time period is a spiritual process.

Although, earlier in his artistic career, he was analyzing objects, he did not feel that the viewer should analyze what one sees, but rather to enjoy it for what it is. This is because the symbolic elements are subjective. As it is written in Hans K. Roethel's book, *Kandinsky*, Kandinsky states on behalf of his own ideology,

After it has been pointed out that addition in art can easily turn into subtraction we now observe the contrary, i.e., (in abstract art) subtraction becomes addition. The eliminated object does not reduce the means of expression but multiplies them infinitely.

This is artistic mathematics-contrasting with mathematics of the sciences. . .

So don't let us try, in problems concerning the arts, to employ methods that begin to lose their values in the sciences. As far as I am concerned, I am happy to know that there can never be 'scientific criteria' to measure quality in art.

At this point in his life, his views are similar to eastern views. Less is more, and now space is more important than objects filling that space or void. He, himself, becomes more spiritually enlightened later in his life.

Conclusion

Spirituality is not the subconscious; it is a part of the inner consciousness in that it is not physically tangible, but one is still aware of it in an outwardly manner. Kandinsky's age was a time when individuals were used to viewing art works that were depictions of objects found in nature. Individuals were not used to viewing objects found in man's inner consciousness, and this was what Kandinsky wanted to share with others. This was not only difficult to convey but even more difficult for the viewer to comprehend because individuals had never viewed such works before. In his book, *Concerning the Spiritual in Art*, Kandinsky again explains how the viewer is too eager to look for a meaning in a picture. He explains,

> *Instead of allowing the inner value of the picture to work, he worries himself in looking for closeness to 'nature,' or 'temperament,' or 'handling,' or 'tonality,' or 'perspective' or what not. His eye does not probe the outer expression to arrive at the inner meaning. In a conversation with an interesting person, we endeavor to get at his fundamental ideas and feelings. We do not bother about the words he uses, nor the spelling of those words, nor the breath necessary for speaking them, nor the movements of his tongue and lips, nor the psychological working on our brain, nor the physical sound in our ear, nor the physiological effect on our nerves. We realize that these things, though interesting and*

important, are not the main things of the moment, but that the meaning and idea is what concerns us. We should have the same feeling when confronted with a work of art. When this becomes general the artist will be able to dispense with natural form and color and speak in purely artistic language.

Kandinsky introduces the viewing of a work of art as a spiritual experience in itself, an experience without any past baggage. His aim was to have the spectator feel the art work, rather than merely viewing the work, just as one would feel a piece of music, rather then viewing the notes on the paper it is written upon. He wanted this even though it is difficult for the viewer to do so because the art work itself is a tangible object, unlike a musical piece filling the air and surrounding the spectator, but he wanted the same result. He wanted the viewer to interact with the art work and allow its energy to effect the viewer emotionally. Kandinsky believed art could be looked upon as a visual deception, causing people to see into things that do not exist. He wanted, rather, that the intangible, the things of the spirit, be more important to human beings than the tangible.

Finally, his later works are not at all morbid; the idea of death is explored and accepted: matter is further dissolved, and the elements of life are transformed into other forms. In his Munich works he captured the energy of nature and he released its dynamic forces on the canvas, exploring his inner tensions and hidden emotions. At the Bauhaus he had evolved a language of signs and symbols expressing philosophical thought in visual terms. In the final years of his life, Kandinsky was able to finally synthesize both his achievements in Munich and at the Bauhaus to express the spiritual in art.

When one studies the progression and transformation of Kandinsky's work, one sees a loosening up of the subject matter, whether it has to do with his working it out, with age or time, or all the experiences in his life. Throughout most of his work, he uses the tools necessary, such as line, form, or color to provoke the viewer to receive a deeper emotional response beyond what one sees visually. Because of his obsession with color, he manipulated this artistic element.

In, *Concerning the Spiritual in Art,* he wrote about his intent of revealing a spirituality in his art. There is a spirituality in his art work which does exist, and as he does this, he uses the terms *'spirit'* and *'soul'* interchangeably. At times the spirit is the originator of the work, while at other times it is the psychological experience. Kandinsky says that the creation of a work of art is the creation of a world. In his mind, the various formulations are not essentially different, since for him the cosmos is permeated with the spirit, and the soul is of a divine and spiritual origin. But Kandinsky also speaks of a *'creative spirit,'* which controls logic and intuition, and elsewhere of the obscurity in which the inner necessity of artistic creation is enveloped; the differentiation between the spirit and the soul becomes progressively closer.

Of course he would think that the spirit and soul were linked and part of one whole. All that is considered good is one, but it was not a simple observation because like his art work, Kandinsky was a complex individual who possessed an abstract mind. It is known that he suffered from periodic states of depression, sometimes imagining he was a victim of persecution, and believing he had to run away because of it. He felt that part of him was closely tied to the invisible, and that life here and in the hereafter, the tangible world and the inner soul, were not opposed. He even believed that one day painters would be able to do without paints or brushes.

It is these kinds of ideas that would have found opposition. Therefore, he may not have just been imagining his persecution, if not from all of society, then from at least the art community. His art work was labeled as, *"Degenerate,"* artwork by Hitler during the war.

In his earlier works, the spiritual aspect exists in the spiritual subject matter. In his later works, his manipulation of specific aspects such as line, color, and placement of objects provokes the spiritual effect on the viewer.

His later works also reveal how, with time and age, Kandinsky viewed his life and felt when the end of his existence was nearing. He did not view it negatively, but on the contrary, he viewed it in a spiritually positive way, which can be seen in his later works. He continued to express his positive spiritual ideals until July of 1944. He died from a stroke on December 13, 1944, in Neuilly-sur-Seine, Paris.

Works Cited

Bovi, Arturo. *Kandinsky*. London: The Hamlyn
    Publishing Group Limited, 1971.
Dearstyne, Howard. *Inside the Bauhaus.*
    NewYork: Rizzoli International
    Publications, 1986.
Feng, Gia-Fu, *Trans. Tao Te Ching*. New York:
    Vintage Books, 1972.
Grohmann, Will. *Wassily Kandinsky: Life and*
    Work. New York: Harry N. Abrams, 1979.
Hahl-Koch, Jelena. *Kandinsky*. New York:
    Rizzoli International Publications, Inc.,
    1993.
Jayakar, Pupul. *Krishnamurti*. San Fransisco:
    Harper & Row, Publishers, 1986.
Kandinsky, Wassily. *Concerning the Spiritual*
    in Art. New York: Dover Publications, 1977.
---------- *Point and Line to Plane*. New York:
    Dover Publications, 1979.
Lacoste, Michel Conil. *Kandinsky*. New York:
    Crown Publishers, 1979.
Lassaigne, Jacques. *Kandinsky*. Geneva:
    Editions d'Art Albert Skira, 1964.
Lindsay, Kenneth C. & Vergo, Peter, Ed.
    Kandinsky: Complete Writings on Art. New
    York: Da Capo Press, 1982.
Long, Rose. *Kandinsky: The Development of*
    an Abstract Style. Oxford: Clarendon Press,
    1980.
Naylor, Gillian. *The Bauhaus.* London: Studio
    Vista/Dutton, 1968.

Overy, Paul. *Kandinsky: The Language of the
        Eye*. New York: Praeger Publishers, 1969.
Roethel, Hans K. *Kandinsky*. Oxford: Phaidon
        Press Limited, 1977.
Roters, Eberhard. *Painters of the Bauhaus*.
        New York: Frederick A. Praeger, Publishers,
        1965.
Suzuki, Daitsetz T. *Zen and Japanese Culture*.
        New York: Bollingen Foundation Inc., 1959.
Vezin, Annette and Luc. *Kandinsky and Der
        Blaue Reiter*. Paris: Pierre Terrail, 1982.
Weiss, Peg. *Kandinsky in Munich: The Formative
        Jundendstil Years*. New Jersey: Princeton
        University Press, 1979.

About the Author

Hae Won Shin, B.F.A., M.A. is a professional artist and photographer. Her art works have appeared in numerous galleries and publications and her photographs have been seen in over one hundred journals.

www.ingramcontent.com/pod-product-compliance
Lightning Source LLC
Chambersburg PA
CBHW071113090426
42737CB00013B/2583